**HAL•LEONARD
INSTRUMENTAL
PLAY-ALONG**

CLASSICAL FAVORITES

CELLO

TITLE	COMPOSER	PAGE	CD TRACK
Ave Maria	Schubert	2	1
Blue Danube Waltz	Strauss, Jr.	3	2
Can Can	Offenbach	4	3
Für Elise	Beethoven	5	4
Habanera	Bizet	6	5
La donna è mobile	Verdi	7	6
Largo (from *Xerxes*)	Handel	8	7
Minuet in G	J.S. Bach	9	8
Morning	Grieg	10	9
Ode to Joy (from *Symphony No. 9*)	Beethoven	11	10
Pavane	Fauré	12	11
The Sleeping Beauty Waltz	Tchaikovsky	13	12
Symphony No. 9 ("From the New World")	Dvořák	14	13
Symphony No. 40, First Movement	Mozart	15	14
Triumphal March (from *Aïda*)	Verdi	16	15
A Tuning notes			16

HOW TO USE THE CD ACCOMPANIMENT:
A MELODY CUE APPEARS ON THE RIGHT CHANNEL ONLY. IF YOUR CD PLAYER
HAS A BALANCE ADJUSTMENT, YOU CAN ADJUST THE VOLUME OF THE
MELODY BY TURNING DOWN THE RIGHT CHANNEL.

ISBN 0-634-08569-7

**HAL•LEONARD®
CORPORATION**
7777 W. BLUEMOUND RD. P.O. BOX 13819 MILWAUKEE, WI 53213

Visit Hal Leonard Online at
www.halleonard.com

◆ 1 AVE MARIA

CELLO

By FRANZ SCHUBERT

Molto adagio

❷ BLUE DANUBE WALTZ

CELLO

By JOHANN STRAUSS, JR.

Tempo di Valse
Orchestra

❸ CAN CAN
from ORPHEUS IN THE UNDERWORLD

CELLO

By JACQUES OFFENBACH

◆④ FÜR ELISE

CELLO

By LUDWIG VAN BEETHOVEN

◆5 HABANERA

CELLO

By GEORGES BIZET

LA DONNA È MOBILE

from RIGOLETTO

CELLO

By GIUSEPPE VERDI

❼ LARGO

from XERXES

CELLO

By GEORGE FRIDERIC HANDEL

❽ MINUET IN G
from the ANNA MAGDALENA NOTEBOOK

CELLO

By JOHANN SEBASTIAN BACH

◆⑨ MORNING
from PEER GYNT

CELLO

By EDVARD GRIEG

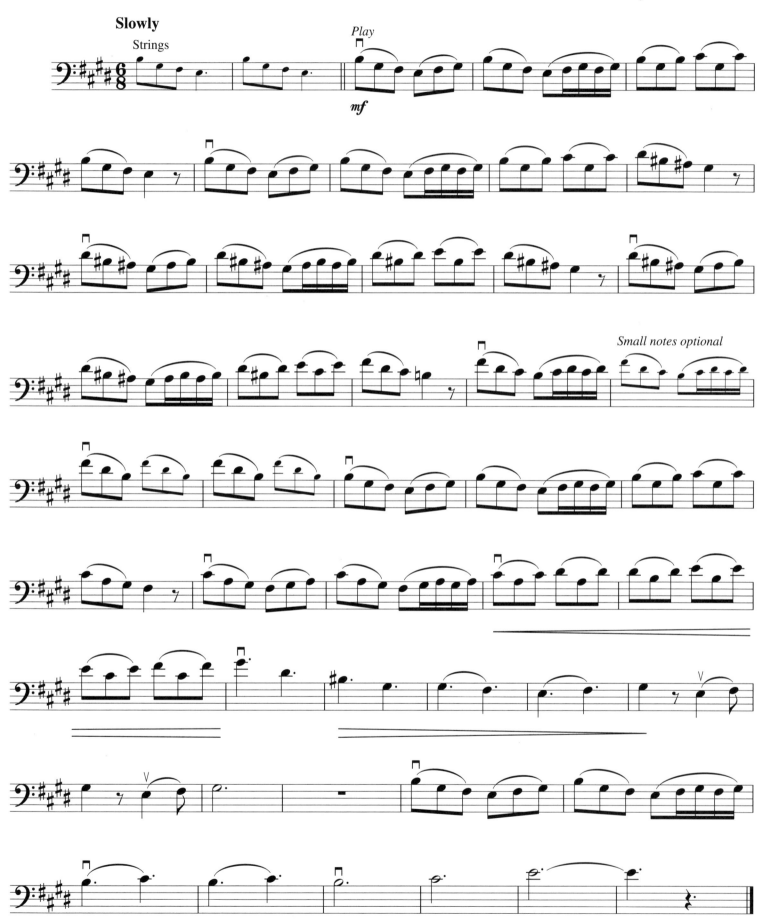

◆ ODE TO JOY

from SYMPHONY NO. 9 IN D MINOR

Words by HENRY VAN DYKE
Music by LUDWIG VAN BEETHOVEN

CELLO

◆11 PAVANE

CELLO

By GABRIEL FAURÉ

12 THE SLEEPING BEAUTY WALTZ

CELLO

By PYOTR IL'YICH TCHAIKOVSKY

◆13 SYMPHONY NO. 9 IN E MINOR

SECOND MOVEMENT EXCERPT

("FROM THE NEW WORLD")

By ANTONÍN DVOŘÁK

CELLO

SYMPHONY NO. 40 IN G MINOR
FIRST MOVEMENT EXCERPT

CELLO

By WOLFGANG AMADEUS MOZART

TRIUMPHAL MARCH

from AÏDA

CELLO

By GIUSEPPE VERDI